I am Preparing for my First Confession

Original Text
Marie-Paule
Mordefroid
with Catechist Team

English Translation by
John McCollough
Jean-Claude Selvini

Illustrations
Christelle Fargue

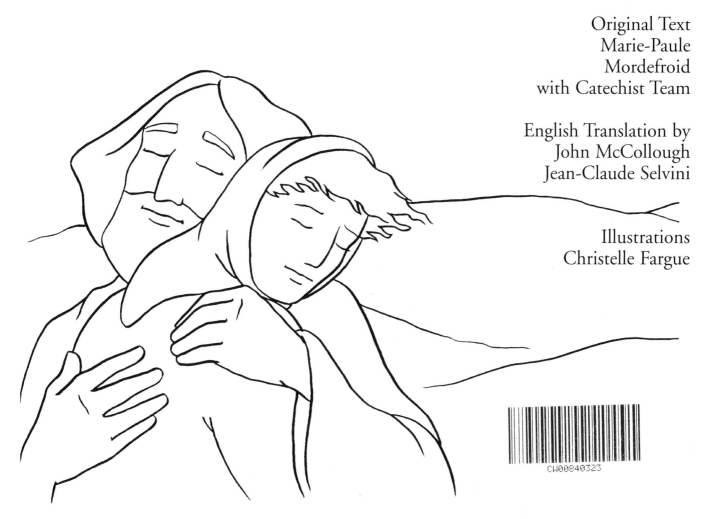

McCrimmons
Great Wakering, Essex

God is Love, He is our Father

God knows each one of us by our name.

He loves us with much tenderness.

He has put His life within us, and He takes care of us.

Mummy and Daddy love us and yet God loves us even more.

He always loves us.

He is our Father and we are His children.

You can complete this prayer:

For the sun and for the trees, thank You Lord!
For water and for the flowers, thank You Lord!
For . . . .
For my family and my friends,
For . . . .
thank You Lord!

At my Baptism you put Your life within me.
I became Your child and I know You love me.
For that love which You put into my heart.
For . . . .
thank You Lord!

Father, help me to love everyone that I
meet, and to love You everyday of my life.

It is difficult to love

We try to love those with whom we live: our parents, our brothers and sisters, our friends, but there are times when it is difficult. Sometimes we disobey our parents, we fight or quarrel with our friends, we tell lies or we say unkind things.
When we feel very unhappy we feel that God's love is no longer in our heart.

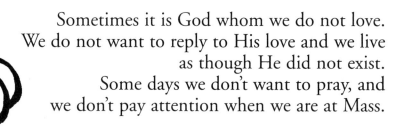

Sometimes it is God whom we do not love. We do not want to reply to His love and we live as though He did not exist.
Some days we don't want to pray, and we don't pay attention when we are at Mass.

When we do what is not pleasing to God, we commit a sin, we turn away from His love.

But God, our Father, does not leave us alone with our sin. He carries on loving us in spite of our faults, and He wants us to turn back to Him.

Bless the Lord, my soul,
and do not forget all his kindness –
who forgives all your faults,
who heals all your diseases.
He surrounds you with love and
tenderness.

The Lord is tenderness and pity,
slow to become angry and full love.
He does not treat us as our faults
deserve,
He does not repay us for our sins.

The love of the Lord for His
children lasts forever.
Bless the Lord, my soul.

(Part of Psalm 103)

Jesus, the Son of God, came to live among us

So that we might know the love
which God has for each of us
God sent us His only Son,
His Son Whom He loves very much,
His Son Who has been with Him forever.
What Jesus did and said shows us
how God the Father loves everyone –
above all sick people and sinners.

*God so loved the world that
He gave His only Son, so that
everyone who believes in Him
may not perish but may have
eternal life.*

John 3: 16

*And all in the crowd were trying to
touch Him, for power came out of
Him and healed all of them.*

Luke 6: 19

Jesus healed many sick people

Jesus ate with sinners

"I have come to call sinners to repentance" Luke 5: 32

Jesus forgave sinners

"Your sins are forgiven" Luke 7: 48

But Jesus wanted everybody to know the mercy of God for each one of us.

The mercy of God – that is, that tender love that He has for each one of us – a love which loves forever without ever getting tired – a love which forgives all our faults.

…So Jesus told the story of the Prodigal Son.

The Parable of the Prodigal Son

Luke 15: 11-32

*A man had two sons. The youngest said to his father:
"Father, give me my share of the inheritance which will
come to me." And the father gave him his share.*

*A few days later,
the younger son collected
together his belongings and
his fortune and left for a far-off
country where he wasted all his
money on having a good time*

*At last he didn't even have
enough to buy something to eat.
So he had to get a job on a
farm looking after pigs.
He was so hungry he would
have eaten the pig-swill if he
could have got it. But no-one
gave him anything.*

Then he began to think. "What a fool I am!" he said to himself. "Even the men who only work for my father have as much as they want to eat. And here am I, starving to death. I'm going back home to my father! I'll tell him that I'm sorry and ask him to treat me as one of his workers."

So he went home again to his father.

His father saw him coming and he felt sorry for the boy.

He ran out to meet him, embraced him and made him welcome. The boy began to say, "Father, I have sinned against heaven and against you – I am no longer worthy to be called your son."

But the father told his servants to get some fresh clothes for the boy and to get a meal ready. "We are going to have a feast," he said, "because I thought my son was dead but now he is alive again, and I have found him once more." And they began to celebrate.

Jesus loves me and He gave Himself for me

To free us from sin, Jesus gave
His life by dying on the cross.
Because of His love for His Father
and because of His love for us
He gave Himself.

"There is no greater love than to give one's life for those whom one loves."

John 15: 13

By raising Jesus from the dead, God shows
that His love is stronger even than death,
stronger than sin.
In the risen Jesus we see the love of God
our Father.

I am Preparing
for my First Confession

Preparation for First Reconciliation is an important event in the life of a child – as much from the point of view of the spiritual life as of ordinary, everyday life. The way in which he / she is prepared to receive this sacrament, the relationship which he /she establishes with God will have bearing for a long time to come.

Thus it is necessary that parents or catechists who are responsible for this preparation should themselves have a positive attitude towards this Sacrament so that they can talk to the children in a positive way with faith and gentleness.

You will find in this pull-out section:

Reconciliation in Salvation History

CONSIDERATION of the mystery of reconciliation between God and mankind in salvation history sheds light on three important aspects of this mystery.
• it is God who takes the initiative
• the mystery is dependent on the Church's ministry
• man must make a response

God's Initiative

The origins of reconciliation are found in the **LOVE OF GOD**. Because God is **LOVE**, He has created mankind in His own image, calling all to live in intimate union with Him and to be brothers and sisters, children of the one Father.

In spite of man's attitude and behaviour, God has remained faithful to His original design. Indeed, man has chosen to turn away from God, seeking to find his own happiness rather than accepting it as a gift from his Creator. This refusal of God's love has brought about great disorders – within man himself, between man and woman, between mankind and the world in which he lives.

But God has never renounced His goodness towards man since He has shown His **MERCY** by sending His Son, Jesus Christ. Jesus, by accepting death on the Cross has brought salvation to man: through Jesus, God is reconciled with man.

The Church's Ministry

After His resurrection Jesus gave the power to remit sins to the Apostles and He sent them the Holy Spirit so that the Good News of Salvation might be proclaimed and received throughout the world. (Jn 20: 19-23)

On the Day of Pentecost, the Church, through the mouth of St. Peter, proclaimed pardon of sins through baptism. Ever since she has not ceased to call man to conversion and to demonstrate the victory of Christ over sin.

In the celebration of the sacraments the Church enables men and women to receive forgiveness of their sins and to live a life reconciled with God. The Sacraments of Baptism, the Eucharist and Reconciliation each show different aspects of this reconciliation of God with man.

Baptism is the first sign of the forgiveness of sins: immersion in the death of Christ, it buries our former nature; a new birth, it enables us to enter into the life of the love of God, Father, Son and Holy Spirit… But the baptised are still at risk from sin, so the Sacrament of Reconciliation allows them to be forgiven anew for their sins committed after baptism.

The Eucharist is the gift of the love of God for Christians who live by His grace. Consequently, the Church requires that whoever has a grave sin on his conscience should not receive Communion until he has received the Sacrament of Reconciliation, for grave sin is a refusal or a disobedience of God and is therefore a breaking of communion with Him.

The Eucharist is also a memorial of the sacrifice of Christ: it enables us personally and communally to participate in the reconciliation gained by Christ. The Council of Trent spoke of the Eucharist as an *"antidote through which we are delivered from daily sins and preserved from grave sins"*

The Sacrament of Reconciliation gives to the baptised the grace to be reconciled with God through forgiveness of sins committed since Baptism. It is the meeting between God's initiative and man's response: God's initiative whereby through His mercy He grants pardon and man's response whereby, confronted with the love of God, he acknowledges his sin and decides to return to his Father and to live in communion with Him and with his brothers and sisters.

Man's Response

Confronted by that merciful love which is revealed and given to all the baptised through Jesus Christ, the Christian is led:

*   to be aware of his **SIN**
*   to turn afresh to God **(CONVERSION)**
*   to be sorry for his sin **(CONTRITION)**
*   to manifest the desire to live a new life **(PENANCE)**

The Christian having received new life in God through Baptism, is not always faithful: sometimes he refuses to respond to the love of God, he lacks determination to accomplish the will of God, preferring to be his own master.

So a radical conversion is necessary. One's whole being should be turned anew towards the Father. One can then approach the holiness of God who will bring his grace to bear to lead the penitent into the fullness of truth.

These two interior dispositions correspond to the two aspects of **CONVERSION** which are in evidence in the Parable of the Prodigal Son: 'he came to himself' and 'he decided to return to his father…'

For a sincere conversion of heart, the Christian who recognises that he has sinned and who desires to restore his relationship with God must have a real **REGRET** for the sins that he has committed and must have the resolve not to sin again with the help of God's grace on account of that renewed love which he has for God.

Finally, conversion of the heart must show itself in concrete ways by daily acts of penitence. These efforts that the Christian makes with the help of God allows him to 'put off the old nature and clothe himself again with the new'. It is the way of life, new in itself, which brings him to be reconciled with God, with himself and with his brothers and sisters.

In preparation of children for the Sacrament of Reconciliation, one must take into account the principal aspects which have been referred to and include them all. For they will provide the basis for an ongoing catechesis which can be adapted according to the age of the children and which will help them to progress in the matter of being reconciled with God.

Conversion, Penance, Pardon Reconciliation

Each one of these words can, in a certain way, be used to define the matter of the Sacrament; but it is important to realise that each word, on it's own does not give an adequate expression.

Conversion marks first of all a radical redirection in one's life.

Penance expresses those deeds of man through which the conversion in one's life operates and bears fruit.

Pardon recalls the initiative of God who is merciful.

Reconciliation is the ultimate goal and the result of the whole process – renewed friendship between God and man.

To speak only of conversion or penance would concentrate on man's efforts. On the other hand, to speak only of pardon risks the idea that here is a gift of God which comes in spite of any efforts of man. Finally to speak only of reconciliation would imply that this is something which we obtain and not necessarily the end of the process.

To be reconciled it is not sufficient that God wishes to forgive the sinner; it is not sufficient that the sinner is sorry for what he has done; pardon and repentance must go hand in hand.

Extract from 'The New Rite of Penance'
December 1993

Jesus and the little children

People were bringing even infants to Him that He might touch them and when the disciples saw it, they sternly ordered them not to do it, But Jesus called for them and said, "Let the little children come to me, and do not stop them; for it is to such as these that the Kingdom of God belongs. Truly I tell you, whoever does not receive the Kingdom of God as a little child will never enter it.

Luke 18: 15-17

At what time may a child receive the Sacrament of Reconciliation?

One cannot answer this question simply by stating a particular age; every child is unique, and it would be regrettable were we to lay down norms which dictated the spiritual development of children.

However, one can recognise that a child is ready to receive the Sacrament when one is aware of the signs of a personal relationship with the Lord together with a sense of good and evil.

The life of faith shows itself in a child by his desire for personal prayer and his desire to do that which is pleasing to God.

The sense of good and evil exists very early on in a child's life and he should be helped to choose the good even if it requires some effort. Such acts performed in early years will be a determining factor for the rest of his life.

Inasmuch as parents know that children have the need to be forgiven for something which they have done wrong, so it is the same in our relationship with God. For young children to be pardoned and forgiven their sins is a source of security and profound joy. The Sacrament of Reconciliation lived out in a climate of trust is an important step in the education of a child's conscience.

Some advice to parents and catechists

The attitude of parents and catechists is of the utmost importance in helping the children to make progress. We have to encourage them with a great deal of compassion and prepare them in an atmosphere of trust in the merciful love of God.

All those preparing children for Reconciliation must display a great respect for their conscience – we must help them with a lot of discretion.

In assisting children to grow in the knowledge of good and evil, we must be on our guard against 'moralising' and from using the Sacrament badly when confronted with difficulties in their lives.

Finally, let us not accord the same gravity to every act committed by a child. There is a difference between an act done on impulse and an act committed after serious thought.

Suggestions for the use of this booklet

⊃ **God is Love and He is our Father** (pp 2 & 3)

The object of this first lesson is to help the children to deepen their discovery of **God the Father's** love for each one of us. This love is shown in:
• the world of nature which surrounds them
• life which is given them
• the love of their parents and their friends
• the desire for beauty and truth which is in their hearts

The discovery that all this comes from God introduces children to prayers of thanksgiving and allows them to understand that they are called to share with others that love which they themselves have received.
The most wonderful gift that they receive is that of the life of a child of God which they receive through Baptism. The Sacrament of Reconciliation gives them back that life of love with God which is weakened by sin.

⊃ **It is difficult to love** (pp 4 & 5)

Confronted with the love of God and with what that love demands, the child begins to understand that he is a sinner, that is to say that he does not always do what God wants him to do.

Different aspects become apparent in this education of conscience as regards a sinful character and the existence of sin.
• In speaking of concrete examples in our daily lives, one can show the children that through their consciences they are capable of telling the difference between good and evil and that, in spite of this being the case, sometimes they choose in certain situations either not to do what is good or, indeed, to do what is evil
• One can also show them that in not loving others, they are offending God who is the creator and Father of all.

• One should help the children to understand that the consequence of sin is to cut us off from God's love and the love of others. On the other hand, being reconciled personally with God gives also the communal dimension of being reconciled with others.

• This awareness of sin should be tied in with the assurance that God continues to love us. With Psalm 103 (102) one can help the children to open their hearts to the love of God who offers them pardon for their sins and gives them a new heart with which to love.

⊃ Jesus the Son of God came amongst us (pp 6 & 7)

During this lesson one can show the children the primary reason for Jesus coming to live with us – to make God's love known to everyone.

One can find out what the children already know about Jesus and then lead into those actions and words regarding sick and sinful people (welcome and compassion; healing and forgiveness of sin). For this one can use readings from the Gospel using the particular references quoted on pages 6 & 7.

⊃ The Parable of the Prodigal Son (pp 8-11)

Jesus told this parable in order to show how God awaits the return of the sinner, forgives his sins and restores his position as a son. But it also casts light on the way in which a sinful person should behave when that person desires to return to God. One will stress

• the behaviour of the father: his words, his gestures and his feelings and desires
• the stages in the decision-making of the son
• the joy of reconciliation and the way in which that joy is expressed, (it is important to notice that it is the father who is the first to rejoice).

It is important to take time to allow the children to understand that this story applies to everyone – it is, in fact, their own story.

In giving them ways of applying this parable to themselves, they will be able to enter more easily into the process of a true and deep reconciliation.

Colouring the drawings, miming the story, puppets, adaptation of the parable are all ways which can help the children identify themselves with the prodigal son, depending on their abilities and what they enjoy doing.

One will note that the true sin of the son is to be separated from his father which then brought about the disordered life which he had to endure.

With the children one will look for examples in their lives in which they can recognise *'disorder'* and unhappiness because they have turned away from God's love. The steps in the development in the son's thinking are used again in the more immediate preparation for the Sacrament of Reconciliation beginning on page 16.

⊃ Jesus loved me and He gave Himself for me (p 12)

This lesson is the second aspect of the coming of Jesus among men: by His death and resurrection Christ has conquered evil, he has freed mankind from sin and has given all the possibility of living anew in the life of God.

One will speak to the children of the death of Jesus, stressing that He gave His life because of His love for us. He loves His Father and He loves us all: through His death on the Cross, mankind has been reconciled with God. With Saint Paul, each person can say again when thinking about Jesus: *'He loved me and gave himself for me'*.

As far as the Resurrection of Jesus is concerned, it is the assurance to us that we can now live the life of God and fight against evil with the help of God the Holy Spirit.

⊃ Those whose sins you forgive, they are forgiven (p 13)

This passage from Saint John's Gospel is important because it shows the connection between Jesus who Himself forgave sins because He is the Son of God, and the Apostles, to whom Jesus gave the power to forgive sins. It is the moment of the institution of the Sacrament of Reconciliation. The Apostles, then their successors the bishops and priests, truly stand in the place of Jesus when they forgive sins in the Name of the Father and of the Son and of the Holy Spirit.

On the other hand, God's forgiveness is granted to mankind in the power of the Holy Spirit: Jesus has died and risen from the dead, the Holy Spirit can now be given to men and women for their sanctification.

⟩ The Sacrament of Reconciliation (pp 14 & 15)

These two pages suggest a reflection and some prayers based on the passage from Saint John's Gospel, read on the previous page. They are suitable for children aged 8-10 who can study the Sacrament in depth, the role of God the Holy Spirit and the connection with their Baptism.

⟩ Preparation for the Sacrament of Reconciliation (pp16-18)

After progressing towards reconciliation with God, these three pages now propose an examination of Conscience, using words of Holy Scripture, as a more immediate preparation for the Sacrament.
It will perhaps be necessary to explain the texts which are at the head of each section. But it is of the utmost importance that there should be great discretion exercised in this particular exercise and absolute respect for the privacy of each child.
One can suggest that the child memorises the Scripture text which has most affected him and uses it at the beginning of his confession during the Sacrament.

⟩ Celebration of the Sacrament of Reconciliation (pp 19 & 20)

It is important that the children should be made aware of the procedure of the Sacrament, that they understand the meaning of the gestures and words of the priests and that they should have learned the prayers which they have to say.
One will recall the role of the priest (how he represents Jesus and also that he is a representative of the Whole Church), the secrecy of the confessional (the seal) to which he is bound, and one should encourage to the children that they should pray for the priest to whom they are going to make their confession.
The celebration of this sacrament should be done in an atmosphere of reflection and trust. It should end with an expression of joy in the reconciliation with God which has been achieved. For example, it is a good idea to have a simple little party with the group of children who have celebrated the sacrament.

Bibliography

Other related titles for First Confession, First Communion and Confirmation available from **McCrimmon Publishing Co. Ltd.**

My Prayer Book for First Holy Communion
Michael Hollings
ISBN 0 85597 557 1

My Prayer Book for Confirmation
Michael Hollings
ISBN 0 85597 558 X

Celebrating Our Faith Series
From Harcourt Religion Publishing

Eucharist Children's Book*
ISBN 0 15950 447 3

Reconciliation Children's Book*
ISBN 0 15950 458 9

* These publications represent only a small part of the *Celebrating Our Faith* series.
For more information on this series or for any of the publications on this page please contact:
McCrimmon Publishing Co. Ltd, 10-12 High St, Great Wakering, Essex SS3 0EQ

Tel   (01702) 218956
Fax   (01702) 216082
Email   mccrimmons@dial.pipex.com
Web   www.mccrimmons.com

Those whose sins you forgive, they are forgiven

On the evening of Easter Day, the disciples had locked the doors of the house where they were because they were afraid they might be arrested like Jesus. But Jesus came straight in and said *"Peace be with you."* He showed them His hands and His side. The disciples were full of joy to see Him once more. Then Jesus said to them again *"Peace be with you. As my Father sent me, so I am sending you."* Having said that, He breathed on them and said,

"Receive the Holy Spirit. Those whose sins you forgive, they will be forgiven; those whose sins you retain, they will be retained."

John 20: 19-23

The Sacrament of Reconciliation

When Jesus gave His Apostles the power to forgive sins, He gave a great gift to us all; from that day onwards every person who wishes it can have his sins forgiven through receiving the Sacrament of Reconciliation and he can be reconciled with God.

While Jesus lived on earth amongst us, He forgave the sins of many people.

Today He continues to forgive sins using a priest as an intermediary who extends his hand while saying the words of absolution to those who come to ask for forgiveness.
(see page 20)

Thank You, Lord Jesus, for the Sacrament of Reconciliation which You have given to Your Church.

Lord Jesus, when I receive this Sacrament, help me to love God our Father and other people more and more.

So that our reconciliation with God might be achieved, and our hearts filled anew with the love of God and the light which that love brings, Jesus sent the Holy Spirit.

The Spirit of Truth and Love came to the Church on the Feast of the Pentecost. Ever since, He helps us to recognise our sins and, at the same time, He reminds us that Jesus has saved us by His death and resurrection.

Come, Holy Spirit, and light up the eyes of my heart. Spread the love of God through the hearts of all people. Change my heart of stone into a heart of flesh.

From the Day of our Baptism, the Holy Spirit lives in our hearts. He helps us live in the love of God. Through Him we can love God and our fellow men. He helps us fight against sin and to come back to God to receive His forgiveness.

Preparation for the Sacrament of Reconciliation

"The son began to think"

Like the prodigal son, I cut myself off from God: I didn't know how to love, I have refused to do His will. But I do not want to live my life separated from God – His love draws me, I am sorry for my sins, I want to go back to my Father.

God is waiting for you; just as the father waited for his prodigal son, God is looking out for your return. He loves you in spite of your faults. He calls you back to Him and He comes to meet you where you are.

It is in the Sacrament of Reconciliation that you live this meeting with God – He forgives you all your sins, He gives you a new heart to love even more and you will be happy.

To prepare to receive forgiveness for your sins, you must take time to look at yourself – just as the prodigal son looked at himself – and to see where you haven't loved God and others. It is by listening to the word of God that we can find out where we have gone wrong – discover our sins:
Jesus tells us how we are to love God our Father and how we are to love others.

I have sinned against God

"You must love the Lord your God with all heart, all your soul and all your mind."
Have I loved God: have I tried to show Him that I love Him by praying to Him and by doing good things for Him?

"When you pray, don't gabble like the pagans."
When I pray, do I speak to God as though I love Him or do I just gabble through my prayers and hymns without thinking about what I'm saying?

"Blessed are those who hear the word of God and put it into practice."
When I am at Mass do I listen carefully to the Word of God in the Scripture readings?
When the Word of God says something to me, do I try to live it out each day?

"Whoever eats my flesh and drinks my blood will have eternal life."
Do I think of the Mass as a meeting with Jesus?
Am I attentive to Him when I receive Holy Communion

I have sinned against others

"Love one another as I have loved you."
Have I loved my parents, my brothers and sisters, by doing what I am told to do, by helping them, by making them happy, by lending and sharing?

"You also must wash one another's feet."
Do I really help others even when I want to do other things?"

"May your yes be yes."
   Have I always told the truth?
   Have I cheated?

"Blessed are those who work for peace."
   Have I avoided fighting with others or have I caused a fight or quarrel?

"Do not judge and you will not be judged."
   Have I been critical of others?
   Have I made fun of others?

"Forgive us our sins as we forgive those who sin against us."
   Have I forgiven others who have hurt me?

I recognise that I have sinned against myself

"Wicked, lazy servant."
   Have I used the gifts / talents that God has given me?

"Whoever abases himself will be exalted."
   Have I been boastful?
   Have I always looked for the most important place?

"Always be joyful."
   Have I been moody or miserable?
   Have I been sulky?

> *Have mercy on me, God.*
> *In your kindness wipe away my pain.*
>
> Psalm 51

Celebration of the Sacrament of Reconciliation

So he went home again

① You go to the priest who represents Jesus. He welcomes you in the name of Jesus. You carefully make the sign of the Cross and say:

"In the name of the Father, and of the Son, and of the Holy Spirit."

and then

"Bless me, Father, for I have sinned."

② You can tell the priest the words of Scripture which have helped you in your preparation.

(3) You recognise that you have sinned by using this prayer

I confess to Almighty God and to you, Father, that I have sinned through my own fault, in my thoughts and in my words, in what I have done and in what I have failed to do; and I ask Blessed Mary, ever virgin, all the angels and saints, and you, Father, to pray for me to the Lord our God.

His father ran out to meet him, embraced him and made him welcome.

You then confess to the priest your sins for which you are asking forgiveness of God to the priest.

When you have finished, the priest speaks to you in the name of Jesus and he asks you to do something particular (a PENANCE), to show the Lord that you wish to do better.

Listen carefully so that you will remember what you have been asked to do.

④ You prepare to receive God's forgiveness by saying this act of contrition or another which you like.

> O my God, I thank you for loving me. I am sorry for all my sins, for not loving others and not loving you. Help me to live like Jesus, and not to sin again. Amen.

The priest extends his hand and gives you the absolution **(GOD'S FORGIVENESS)**

God, the Father of mercies, through the death and resurrection of his Son has reconciled the world to Himself and sent the Holy Spirit among us for the forgiveness of sins, through the ministry of the Church may God give you pardon and peace, and I absolve you from your sins in the name of the Father, and of the Son, and of the Holy Spirit.

Amen.

They began to celebrate.

(5) You are happy to have your sins forgiven and the priest invites you to say thank you to God.

Go in the peace and joy of Christ.

Blessed be God, now and forever.

Let us give thanks to the Lord
for He is good
and His love lasts forever!

The Lord has saved us:
we called to Him and He delivered,
us from our sin.

Let us give thanks to the Lord for His love,
for the wonders He does for us:
He has given good things to the hungry.

Let us offer sacrifices of thanksgiving,
let us proclaim His wonderful works.

Let us give thanks to the Lord
for He is good
and His love lasts forever!
Alleluia!

From Psalm 107

23

First published in France by
Editions de l'Emmanuel
BP 137 – 92 223
Bagneux

English Edition first published in Great Britain in 2000 by
McCrimmon Publishing Co. Ltd.
10-12 High Street, Great Wakering, Essex, SS3 0EQ
Telephone   (01702) 218956
Fax   (01702) 216082
Email   mccrimmons@dial.pipex.com
Web   www.mccrimmons.com

ISBN 0 85597 619 5

Cum Permissu Superium: Fr. Alain Houry, FEC
                                                          Visiteur Paris-Rouen
Nihil Obstat: Fr. George Stokes, Censor Deputatus
Imprimatur: Mgr. William Nix, Vic. Gen.

Although the publication is free from doctrinal error it does not necessarily reflect the views of those who have granted the Nihil Obstat and Imprimatur

The English translation of the Order of Mass from *The Roman Missal* © 1973, ICEL

Illustrations and cover artwork by Christelle Fargue
Page design and layout by Brendan Waller
Printed and bound by Thanet Press Ltd, Margate, Kent